OCARINA SONGS
FOR ALL OCCASIONS

ARRANGED BY CRIS GALE

2 Abide with Me
2 Amazing Grace
3 America, the Beautiful
4 Angels We Have Heard on High
3 Auld Lang Syne
4 Aura Lee
6 Christ the Lord Is Risen Today
6 Danny Boy
5 Deck the Halls
5 Fum, Fum, Fum
7 Greensleeves
8 Hail to the Chief
12 Happy Birthday to You
8 Hava Nagila (Let's Be Happy)
9 Jingle Bells

10 Joy to the World
11 Marine's Hymn
10 My Country, 'Tis of Thee (America)
11 My Dreidel
14 O Come, All Ye Faithful
12 The Old Rugged Cross
13 Pomp and Circumstance
14 Sevivon
15 The Star-Spangled Banner
18 Up on the Housetop
18 We Shall Overcome
19 Wedding March (Bridal Chorus)
16 When Irish Eyes Are Smiling
16 When the Saints Go Marching In
17 You're a Grand Old Flag

ISBN 978-1-5400-7045-6

Copyright © 2021 by HAL LEONARD LLC
International Copyright Secured   All Rights Reserved

Visit Hal Leonard Online at
www.halleonard.com

Contact us:
Hal Leonard
7777 West Bluemound Road
Milwaukee, WI 53213
Email: info@halleonard.com

In Europe, contact:
Hal Leonard Europe Limited
42 Wigmore Street
Marylebone, London, W1U 2RN
Email: info@halleonardeurope.com

In Australia, contact:
Hal Leonard Australia Pty. Ltd.
4 Lentara Court
Cheltenham, Victoria, 3192 Australia
Email: info@halleonard.com.au

2

ABIDE WITH ME

Words by HENRY F. LYTE
Music by WILLIAM H. MONK

AMAZING GRACE

Words by JOHN NEWTON
Traditional American Melody

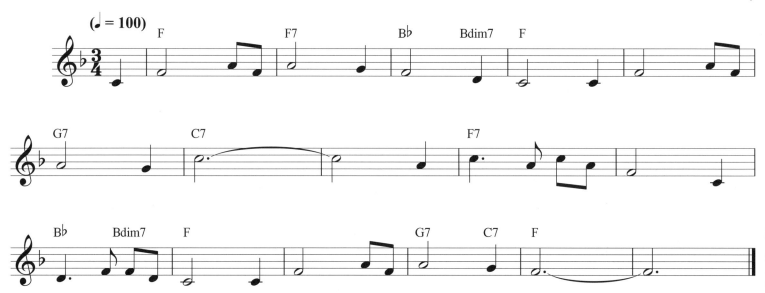

AMERICA, THE BEAUTIFUL

Words by KATHARINE LEE BATES
Music by SAMUEL A. WARD

AULD LANG SYNE

Words by ROBERT BURNS
Traditional Scottish Melody

ANGELS WE HAVE HEARD ON HIGH

Traditional French Carol
Translated by JAMES CHADWICK

AURA LEE

Words by W.W. FOSDICK
Music by GEORGE R. POULTON

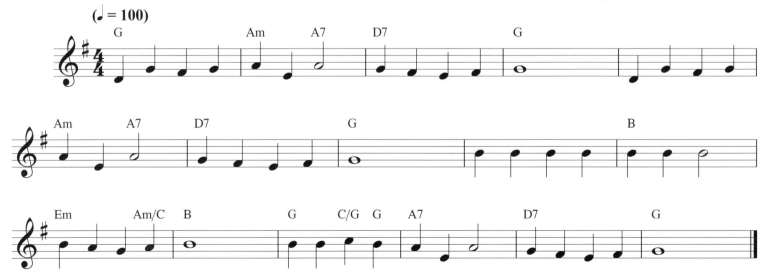

DECK THE HALLS

Traditional Welsh Carol

FUM, FUM, FUM

Traditional Catalonian Carol

CHRIST THE LORD IS RISEN TODAY

Words by CHARLES WESLEY
Music adapted from *Lyra Davidica*

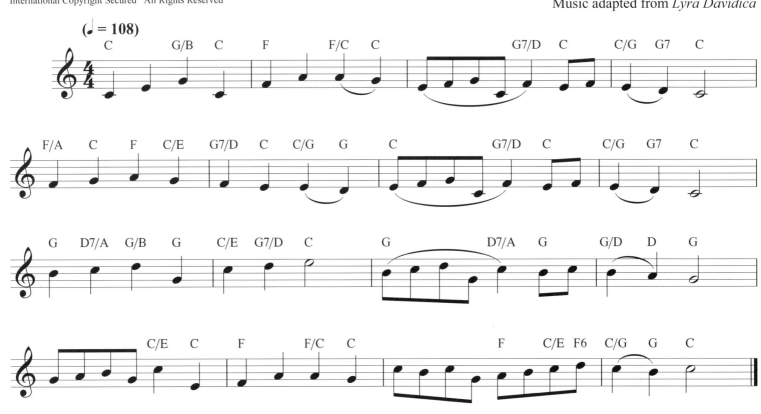

DANNY BOY

Words by FREDERICK EDWARD WEATHERLY
Traditional Irish Folk Melody

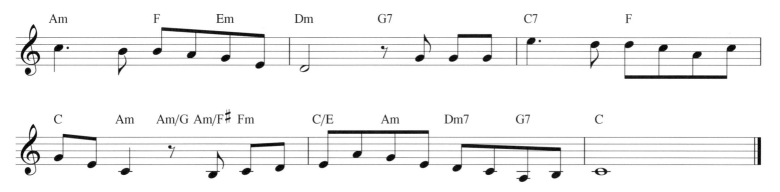

GREENSLEEVES

Sixteenth Century Traditional English

HAIL TO THE CHIEF

By JAMES SANDERSON

HAVA NAGILA
(Let's Be Happy)

Lyrics by MOSHE NATHANSON
Music by ABRAHAM Z. IDELSOHN

JINGLE BELLS

Words and Music by
J. PIERPONT

JOY TO THE WORLD

Words by ISAAC WATTS
Music by GEORGE FRIDERIC HANDEL

MY COUNTRY, 'TIS OF THEE
(America)

Words by SAMUEL FRANCIS SMITH
Music from *Thesaurus Musicus*

MARINE'S HYMN

Words by HENRY C. DAVIS
Melody based on a theme by JACQUES OFFENBACH

MY DREIDEL

Traditional

HAPPY BIRTHDAY TO YOU

Words and Music by MILDRED J. HILL
and PATTY S. HILL

THE OLD RUGGED CROSS

Words and Music by
REV. GEORGE BENNARD

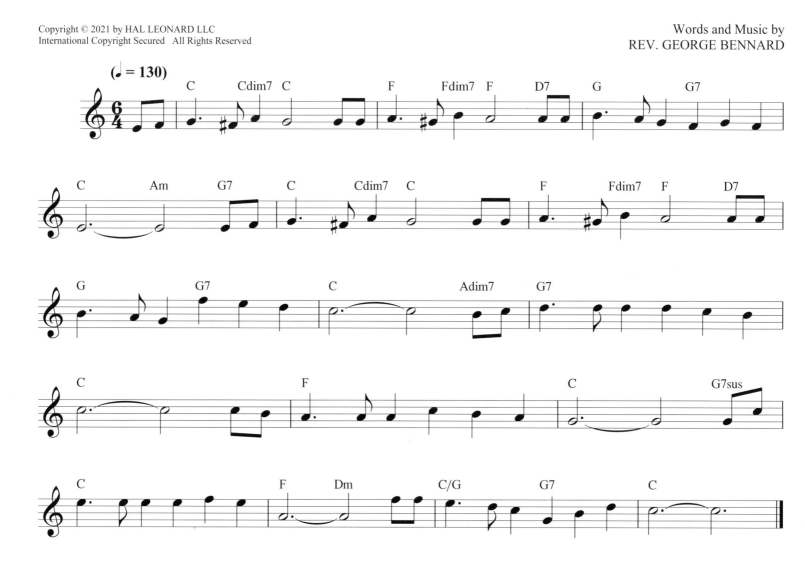

POMP AND CIRCUMSTANCE

Words by ARTHUR BENSON
Music by EDWARD ELGAR

O COME, ALL YE FAITHFUL

Music by JOHN FRANCIS WADE
Latin Words translated by FREDERICK OAKELEY

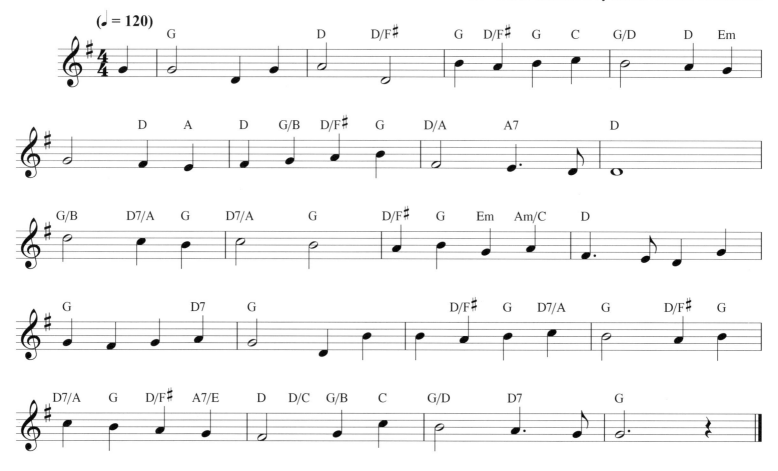

SEVIVON

Traditional Hebrew Chanukah Song

THE STAR-SPANGLED BANNER

Words by FRANCIS SCOTT KEY
Music by JOHN STAFFORD SMITH

WHEN THE SAINTS GO MARCHING IN

Traditional

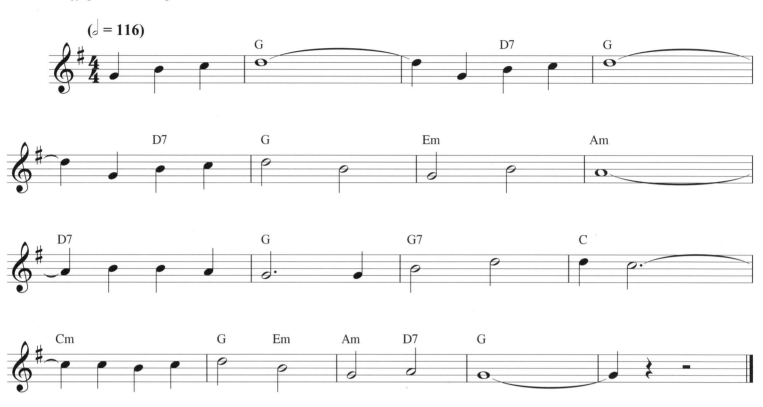

WHEN IRISH EYES ARE SMILING

Words by CHAUNCEY OLCOTT
and GEORGE GRAFF, JR.
Music by ERNEST R. BALL

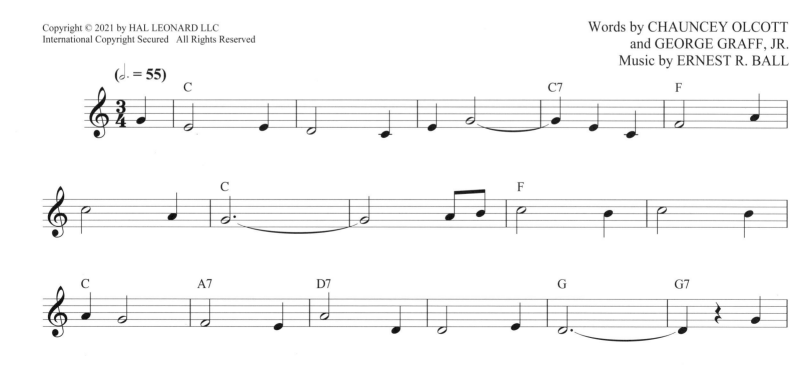

YOU'RE A GRAND OLD FLAG

Words and Music by
GEORGE M. COHAN

UP ON THE HOUSETOP

Words and Music by
B.R. HANBY

WE SHALL OVERCOME

Words based on 1901 hymn by C. ALBERT FINDELY
entitled "I'll Overcome Some Day"
Music based on 1794 hymn entitled "O Sanctissima"

WEDDING MARCH
(Bridal Chorus)

By RICHARD WAGNER

MORE GREAT OCARINA PUBLICATIONS

Christmas Carols for Ocarina
Arranged for 10, 11 & 12-Hole Ocarinas
30 favorite carols of the holiday season: Angels We Have Heard on High • Away in a Manger • Coventry Carol • Deck the Hall • God Rest Ye Merry, Gentlemen • It Came upon the Midnight Clear • Jingle Bells • Joy to the World • O Come, All Ye Faithful • O Holy Night • Silent Night • Up on the Housetop • We Wish You a Merry Christmas • and more.

00277990 ....$9.99

Christmas Favorites for Ocarina
Arranged for 10, 11 & 12-Hole Ocarinas
Play 23 holiday classics in arrangements tailored to this unique wind instrument: Blue Christmas • Christmas Time Is Here • Do You Hear What I Hear • Frosty the Snow Man • Have Yourself a Merry Little Christmas • The Little Drummer Boy • The Most Wonderful Time of the Year • Rockin' Around the Christmas Tree • Silver Bells • White Christmas • Winter Wonderland • and more.

00277989 ....$9.99

Disney Songs for Ocarina
Arranged for 10, 11 & 12-Hole Ocarinas
30 Disney favorites, including: Be Our Guest • Can You Feel the Love Tonight • Colors of the Wind • Do You Want to Build a Snowman? • Evermore • He's a Pirate • How Far I'll Go • Kiss the Girl • Lava • Mickey Mouse March • Seize the Day • That's How You Know • When You Wish Upon a Star • A Whole New World • You've Got a Friend in Me • Zip-A-Dee-Doo-Dah • and more..

00275998 ....$9.99

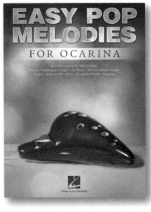

Easy Pop Melodies for Ocarina
Arranged for 10, 11 & 12-Hole Ocarinas
30 popular hits: Believer • City of Stars • Every Breath You Take • Hallelujah • Happy • I'm Yours • The Lion Sleeps Tonight • My Heart Will Go on (Love Theme from *Titanic*) • Perfect • Rolling in the Deep • Shake It Off • Some Nights • The Sound of Silence • Stay with Me • Sweet Caroline • Uptown Girl • What a Wonderful World • Yesterday • You've Got a Friend • and more.

00275999 ....$9.99

Folk Songs for Ocarina
Arranged for 10, 11 & 12-Hole Ocarinass
41 well-known songs: Alouette • Aura Lee • The Banana Boat Song • Follow the Drinkin' Gourd • Frere Jacques (Are You Sleeping?) • Hava Nagila (Let's Be Happy) • Home on the Range • Hush, Little Baby • Joshua (Fit the Battle of Jericho) • Kumbaya • La Cucaracha • Loch Lomond • My Bonnie Lies over the Ocean • My Old Kentucky Home • My Wild Irish Rose • Oh! Susanna • Scarborough Fair • Shenandoah • Swing Low, Sweet Chariot • This Little Light of Mine • Twinkle, Twinkle Little Star • Volga Boatman Song • When Johnny Comes Marching Home • The Yellow Rose of Texas • and more.

00276000...$9.99

Hal Leonard Ocarina Method
by Cris Gale
The Hal Leonard Ocarina Method is a comprehensive, easy-to-use beginner's guide, designed for anyone just learning to play the ocarina. Inside you'll find loads of techniques, tips and fun songs to learn and play. The accompanying online video, featuring author Cris Gale, provides further instruction as well as demonstrations of the music in the book. Topics covered include: a history of the ocarina • types of ocarinas • breathing and articulation • note names and key signatures • meter signatures and rhythmic notation • fingering charts • many classic folksongs • and more.

00146676   Book/Online Video $14.99

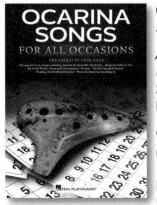

Ocarina Songs for All Occasions
Arranged for 10, 11 & 12-Hole Ocarinas
arr. Cris Gale
30 songs for every season: America, the Beautiful • Auld Lang Syne • Danny Boy • Hail to the Chief • Happy Birthday to You • Joy to the World • The Old Rugged Cross • Pomp and Circumstance • Sevivon • The Star-Spangled Banner • Wedding March (Bridal Chorus) • When the Saints Go Marching In • and more.

00323196...$9.99

WWW.HALLEONARD.COM

Prices, contents, and availability subject to change without notice.
Disney characters and artwork TM & © 2021 Disney